SCIENTIFIC AMERICAN | EDUCATIONAL PUBLISHING

SCIENCE IN THE KITCHEN

10 FUN

PROJECTS USING FOOD

BRING SCIENCE HOME

T004861

Published in 2024 by Scientific American Educational Publishing in association with
The Rosen Publishing Group.

Contains material from Scientific American, a division of Springer Nature America, Inc., reprinted by permission as
well as original material from The Rosen Publishing Group.

Editor: Kristen Rajczak Nelson
Designer: Rachel Rising

Activity on p. 5 by Science Buddies, (April 21, 2016); p. 11 by Science Buddies (May 21, 2015); p. 16 by Science
Buddies, Sabine De Brabandere (January 2, 2020); p. 21 by Science Buddies (March 17, 2016); p. 27 by Science
Buddies (December 25, 2014); p. 33 by Science Buddies (June 20, 2013); p. 38 by Science Buddies, Sabine De
Brabandere (September 28, 2017); p. 44 Science Buddies (October 15, 2015); p. 50 by Science Buddies (April 2,
2015); p. 56 by Science Buddies (July 25, 2013).

All illustrations by Continuum Content Solutions

Photo Credits: pp. 5, 11, 16, 21, 27, 33, 38, 44, 50, 56 Anna Frajtova/Shutterstock.com; pp. 5, 9, 21, 25, 33, 26, 44,
47, 50, 54, 56, 59 cve iv/Shutterstock.com.

Cataloging-in-Publication Data
Names: Scientific American Educational Publishing, editor.
Title: Science in the kitchen : 10 fun projects using food / Scientific
   American.
Description: Buffalo, NY : Scientific American Educational Publishing, an
   imprint of Rosen Publishing, [2024] | Series: Bring science home |
   Includes index.
Identifiers: LCCN 2023026560 (print) | LCCN 2023026561 (ebook) | ISBN
   9781725350069 (paperback) | ISBN 9781725350076 (library binding) | ISBN
   9781725350083 (ebook)
Subjects: LCSH: Food--Experiments--Juvenile literature.
Classification: LCC TX355 .S323 2024 (print) | LCC TX355 (ebook) | DDC
   641.3--dc23/eng/20230623
LC record available at https://lccn.loc.gov/2023026560
LC ebook record available at https://lccn.loc.gov/2023026561

Manufactured in the United States of America

Some of the images in this book illustrate individuals who are models. The depictions do not imply actual
situations or events.

CPSIA Compliance Information: Batch #CWSA24. For further information contact Rosen Publishing, New York, New York at 1-800-237-9932.

Find us on

CONTENTS

⚛ THESE ACTIVITIES INCLUDE
    SCIENCE FAIR PROJECT IDEAS.

INTRODUCTION

Spending time in the kitchen is like spending time in a science lab but with more delicious results! Scientists measure, pour, and create chemical solutions to experiment and test hypotheses. Likewise, cooking, baking, and preserving requires you to follow a recipe and heat up ingredients. But instead of testing theories, you end up with dinner or a treat!

Projects marked with ⚛ include a section called Science Fair Project Ideas. These ideas can help you develop your own original science fair project. Science fair judges tend to reward creative thought and imagination, and it helps if you are really interested in your project. You will also need to follow the scientific method. See page 61 for more information about that.

⚛ How Sour or How Sweet Is It?

LEARN HOW MOLECULES IN OUR FOODS AND DRINKS INTERACT TO MAKE JUST THE RIGHT TASTE WITH THIS ACTIVITY YOU CAN TRY—AND SIP—AT HOME!

PROJECT TIME

🕐 25 to 30 minutes

KEY CONCEPTS

Taste
Acidity
Sugar
Science of cooking

Cooking is a fun and rewarding activity. It allows you to be a cook and scientist at the same time, experimenting with endless taste combinations! The five tastes humans can experience are: sweet, sour, salty, bitter, and umami (savory). But have you ever experienced some combinations that were delicious and others that were downright yucky? How do cooks come up with delicious recipes? And even more amazingly, how can they replicate the same exact flavors over and over again? Does science have anything to do with it? This activity will show how cooking and science can yield a delicious partnership.

5

BACKGROUND

Food has taste because specific chemical particles found in the food activate taste buds in our mouths. Some tastes are created by one specific small particle (such as the hydrogen ion, H^+, for the sour taste) whereas other tastes are activated by several long complex particles (for instance, sucrose, sucralose, and saccharin all induce a sweet taste). Cooks play around with our five tastes to create well-balanced, delicious food. In this activity, you will experience how combining a sweet and sour taste creates an interesting experience.

Cooks use ingredients from nature, such as lemons, which show a natural variability in the amount of taste-inducing particles they contain. One lemon might be more sour than another. How can they reproduce a delicious taste over and over again if their ingredients show variations? The secret lies in the instruments they use. A more scientifically minded cook focuses on precision and prefers more exact instruments rather than the measuring spoons and cups that a typical cook uses. A scale is one example. It measures the mass of sugar, which is directly related to the number of sugar (or sweetness-inducing) particles. Similarly, instead of adding a teaspoon of vinegar to balance a drink's sweetness, a scientifically minded cook might add vinegar until it reaches a specific pH. The pH of a liquid indicates how many hydrogen particles (or sour-inducing particles) are in the liquid. In other words, a pH meter can directly measure the number of sour-inducing particles in a fluid. This allows them to reproduce food that tastes almost exactly the same over and over again.

MATERIALS

- Three glasses
- Water
- Measuring cup
- White crystal sugar
- Measuring spoons that include 1 teaspoon and 1/4 teaspoon
- Mixing and tasting spoons
- White wine vinegar (Other types of vinegar will work, too, but might not provide an equally pleasant taste.)
- Sticky notes or other ways to differentiate the glasses (optional)

PREPARATION

- Differentiate your three glasses; this can be done with sticky notes reading "Sugar Water," "Sugar and Vinegar Water," and "Vinegar Water" or by placing different colored spoons in each glass.

PROCEDURE

- Measure 1 cup (237 ml) of water and add it to the first glass. This will be the glass for sugar water.

- Add 1 teaspoon of sugar to the glass of water and stir until the sugar is dissolved. Taste the sugar-water solution. *Does it taste sweet, pleasantly sweet, or too sweet?*

- Repeat the previous step four more times in the same glass, each time adding 1 more teaspoon of sugar, mixing and tasting. *After how many teaspoons did you find the sugar water had become pleasantly sweet?*

- You have now added a total of 5 teaspoons of sugar. This is approximately 25 grams. *Do you find this amount of sugar in 1 cup of water unpleasantly sweet? Knowing 1 cup (237 ml) of soda has about 25 grams of sugar, why do you think most people find soda tasty but find this sugar water less palatable?*

- Pour half of the sugar water from the first glass into a second glass. Be as precise as you can. This will be the glass for sugar and vinegar water. Set the leftover 1/2 cup (118 ml) of sugar water aside for later.

- Next you will add vinegar to the sugar and water solution, a little bit at a time. *How much vinegar do you think you will need to add before the drink tastes good, or do you think the sugar and vinegar water solution will never taste good?* Now add 1/4 teaspoon (1.2 ml) of vinegar into this second glass, mix, and taste the solution. *How does it taste? Is it better than the pure sugar water?*

- If your solution does not have a pleasing taste yet, add another 1/4 teaspoon (1.2 ml) of vinegar, mix, and taste again. Repeat this step until you get a pleasant tasting solution—but remember to keep track of how much vinegar you added. *Are you surprised about how quickly the sugar water changes taste as you add small amounts of vinegar?*

- Set your sugar and vinegar water solution aside and pour 1/2 cup (118 ml) of water into the third glass. This will be your vinegar water glass.

- Add the same amount of vinegar as you added to the second glass. This is probably one to three 1/4 teaspoon (1.2 ml) additions. Mix the solution and taste. *Is it a pleasant taste?*

ExTRA

Taste is just one aspect of flavor. Smell, texture, and even expectation all contribute to your flavor experience. *What can you add to your pleasant tasting sugar and vinegar water to add more flavor without changing the concentration of sweet-producing and sour-producing agents?* Some suggestions are lemon or orange rind, a slice of cucumber, or even some food coloring.

ExTRA

Check the label of foods like tomato sauce, ketchup, or lemonade, all of which have a major sour component. *Can you find a sweetening component in the ingredient list to balance the sour taste?* You can do the same with recipes in a cookbook at home.

SCIENCE FAIR IDEA

How exactly does a measuring cup or measuring spoon gauge an amount of sugar? Try it out by loosely scooping out 1 cup of sugar and measuring its mass with a scale. Then set aside this sugar and repeat the procedure again, and again. *Do you get exactly the same number on your scale or do you see small variations?* Now repeat this, but press your sugar into the cup (or pack it tightly) and measure the mass of this amount of sugar. Repeat this a few more times to see how much variation you get each time. *What other variations on scooping out a cup of sugar can you think of? Would the type of crystal sugar (for example, coarse versus superfine) make a difference? Which method do you think is most exact in measuring an amount of sweetness-inducing particles—measuring its mass or its volume?*

OBSERVATIONS AND RESULTS

You probably found the sugar water very sweet, the vinegar water too sour, and the water with vinegar and sugar surprisingly tasty.

Our taste has actually evolved to help us detect nutritious foods and avoid foods that are harmful. Sweet, in general, indicates energy and vitamins whereas sour can indicate unripe or rotting. The sweet and sour taste combination appears in many nutritious ripe fruits, such as tomatoes and oranges.

Cooks are experts in creating pleasant-tasting recipes. They know the art of balancing different tastes and how small amounts of sour-inducing particles can balance many more sweet-inducing particles. In your recipe, you probably poured in 1/4 teaspoon (1.2 ml) of vinegar two to three times, which corresponds to adding one sour-inducing particle for every 3,000 to 4,000 sugar particles to obtain a balanced taste.

A spoon or cup measures a volume of an ingredient whereas a scale measures its mass. If you followed the "Extra" instructions, you probably realized how a tightly packed cup of sugar weighs quite a bit more than a loosely packed one does. Because sweetness-inducing particles have a specific mass, measuring the mass of the sugar will provide a more exact number of sugar particles than measuring a cup of sugar, which is why scientifically minded cooks often prefer a scale instead of a measuring cup.

CLEANUP

Pour out the liquids, wash the cups and measuring spoons, and return all materials to where you found them.

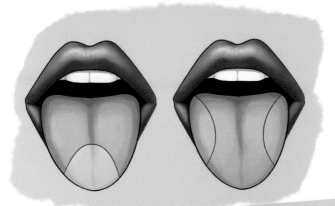

Pucker Up
Sweet and Sour Science

SYNTHETIC OR PURE CANE SUGAR—CAN YOU TELL THE DIFFERENCE? USE THIS ACTIVITY TO FIND OUT WHICH ONE MAKES YOUR LEMONADE SWEETER!

PROJECT TIME
🕐 20 to 30 minutes

KEY CONCEPTS
Food science
Chemistry
Artificial sweeteners
Sugar
Taste

Picture your favorite treats: chocolate fudge cake, vanilla ice cream, pink lemonade . . . Yum! Can you imagine what these might taste like without the sweet flavor of sugar? Your sweet tooth might be aching without the chemical compound of sucrose that is so appealing. Much of the food we eat contains sucrose or natural sweeteners such as honey. There are of course other sweetening options. Have you ever seen "zero-calorie and sugar-free lemonade" at the store and wondered how it was made? Perhaps you've tried sugar-free candy or diet soda. Scientists have developed artificial sweeteners that provide the taste of "sweet" without the sugar itself. How sweet are they? Get ready to make some of your own artificially sweetened lemonade and find out how it compares with lemonade made with real sugar. Prepare yourself for some sour and sweet scientific discovery!

BACKGROUND

Artificial sweeteners are a common substitute for sucrose (sugar). Sucrose is a natural substance, a carbohydrate derived from sugarcane that is used by our bodies for energy. Sucralose, the sweetener in Splenda, is a manufactured alteration of the sucrose molecule. The compound cannot be broken down by the body and therefore is calorie-free. Other artificial sweeteners such as saccharin (in Sweet'n Low) work in the same manner, creating the sweet taste without the calories the body gets from sugar. How sweet are these synthetic compounds compared with sugar? You will test just that as you make your own sugar-free lemonade!

MATERIALS

- Six medium- to large-size lemons (Alternatively, you can buy pure lemon juice at the store.)
- Pure cane sugar (table sugar)
- Water: 2 1/4 cups (532 ml)
- Artificial sweetener (Splenda or Sweet'n Low)
- Three spoons
- One knife
- Three drinking cups
- Strainer
- Bowl
- Permanent marker
- Liquid volume measurer (at least 1 cup [237 ml] volume)
- 1/4 teaspoon measuring spoon
- Volunteer taste testers (optional)
- Additional cups (three for each volunteer) or large spoons (three for each volunteer)

PREPARATION

- To make the lemon juice, slice lemons into four pieces (across the length of the lemon works best) then squeeze the juice into the volume-measuring cup. Squeeze lemons until you have 1 cup (237 ml) lemon juice.

12

- Strain the lemon juice into another plastic cup, and then pour the strained juice back into the liquid volume-measuring cup.

PROCEDURE

- Using the liquid volume-measuring cup, pour 1/4 cup (59 ml) of lemon juice into three different cups.

- Use the liquid volume-measuring cup to add 3/4 cup (177 ml) of water to each cup. Stir the contents of the cups with a spoon to mix the juice with water. *How do you think the plain lemon-and-water drink will taste?*

- Now it's time to add the sweeteners! *Which do you think will make sweeter lemonade—sugar or an artificial sweetener? Why?*

- To the first cup, add no sugar or artificial sweetener.

- To the second cup, add 1/4 teaspoon of pure cane sugar (table sugar). Stir with a spoon until the sugar is entirely dissolved, with none left on the bottom.

- To the third cup, add 1/4 teaspoon of artificial sweetener (Splenda or Sweet'n Low). Stir until the sweetener is entirely dissolved, with none left on the bottom.

- Now it's time for the taste testing! If you have volunteers, you can pour each taste tester a small sample into other cups—or have each person take a large spoonful to taste. Take a small sip of unsweetened lemonade. *What does it taste like? What was your reaction?*

- Take a small sip from the lemonade sweetened with sugar. *What does it taste like?*

- Now take a small sip of the lemonade sweetened with artificial sweetener. *What does this one taste like? How do the two sweetened beverages taste compared with the plain lemon juice? How do they compare with one another?*

- *Overall, which cup had the sweetest lemonade? If you had taste testers, does everyone agree? Which beverage do you (and your volunteers) prefer? Why?*

ExTRA

Can you make lemonade sweetened by sugar and artificial sweetener equal in sweetness? Start with the one that is bitterer and add more of its sweetening substance, in 1/4-teaspoon increments, until it tastes just as sweet as the other lemonade. How much of the substance did you need to add to make the lemonades equal in sweetness? Were you surprised by how much or how little you needed to add?

OBSERVATIONS AND RESULTS ·········

Did you find that the lemonade made with artificial sweetener was sweeter than that made with sugar? Did the original sugar lemonade taste almost as sour and bitter as the pure lemon juice?

Artificial sweeteners are synthetic compounds designed to produce the intense sweet taste you observed in the artificially sweetened lemonade. In fact, the sweetness of artificial sweeteners is many times that of sugar. This means that if you add equal quantities of sugar and an artificial sweetener, the drink with the artificial sweetener will taste sweeter.

If you completed the "Extra" challenge, you may have seen that it took several teaspoons of sugar to equal the sweetness of the artificial sweetener. Splenda is 600 times sweeter than sugar and saccharine, found in Sweet'n Low, is 300 to 500 times sweeter. In the lemonade, some of the sweetness is masked by the sourness of the lemon so you will not need to add 100 more teaspoons of sugar to get the same sweetness as 1/4 teaspoon of sweetener.

Although artificial sweetener does not add additional calories to foods and drinks that use it, we don't know exactly how it works inside our bodies after we consume it, so scientists are still looking into health effects.

CLEANUP ·

Pour out—or drink—the remaining lemonade, and wash the cups and measuring devices. Put the materials back where you found them.

How Warm Is Sweet Enough?

JUST THE RIGHT TASTE—AND TEMPERATURE? LEARN ABOUT HOW OUR BODIES SENSE FLAVOR WITH THIS TASTY ACTIVITY!

Have you ever tasted a piece of warm apple pie or a cup of hot chocolate milk, and then had them after they cooled? Maybe you prefer to have these treats at room temperature. Why is this? Can flavor change even when you are not adding ingredients? Try this activity and discover how temperature affects flavor!

PROJECT TIME

15 to 25 minutes, plus 30 minutes of preparation time

KEY CONCEPTS

Human biology
Senses
Taste
Smell
Food science

BACKGROUND

Our experience with flavor starts in our mouth. There, the particles in food that are responsible for taste activate our taste buds. When these taste buds are triggered, they send a signal to our brain, and we perceive a particular flavor. Humans have thousands of taste buds; they are mainly located on the tip and upper parts of the tongue. They help to distinguish at least five basic tastes: sweet, salty, savory (umami), bitter, and sour—and provide information on the intensity of each of these.

Our experience with flavor does not end in the mouth. It is also influenced by our sense of smell. Food also releases scent particles. When these particles float into our nose, they activate our smell receptors. These receptors send a signal to our brain, and we perceive a particular smell. Humans have several million specialized smell receptors; they are mainly located in our nasal cavity. When food is heated, it releases a burst of these particles. That is why you can easily smell the delicious pie baking in the oven or a hearty soup cooking on the stove.

Our brain combines the signals from our taste buds with those received from our smell receptors to produce the broad sensation of flavor that we are familiar with. Scientists have found that taste buds work more efficiently at warmer temperatures than at colder ones. Does that make us perceive the flavor of warm food more intensely? Try this activity to find out!

MATERIALS

- Ice cream
- Two small bowls
- Spoon
- Two pieces of milk chocolate
- Freezer
- Glass of water
- Volunteers (optional)
- Milk or chocolate milk (optional)
- Two mugs (optional)
- Microwave or stovetop (optional)
- A bitter- or sour-tasting food or drink, such as unsweetened tea, lemonade, and so on (optional)

PREPARATION

- At least half an hour before you start the activity, place one piece of milk chocolate in the freezer. Leave the other piece out at room temperature.

- Scoop a small amount of ice cream into a bowl, and leave it out at room temperature. Return the rest of the ice cream to the freezer.

- Do not consume sugary or strongly flavored food in the half hour before you start the activity.

PROCEDURE

- Remove the piece of chocolate from the freezer. Break off a small piece, and leave the rest in the freezer.

- Place the small, cold piece on your tongue. Close your mouth and concentrate on the flavor. *What does the chocolate taste like?*

- Let the chocolate melt in your mouth. *Does the flavor change as the chocolate melts? When is the flavor of chocolate the strongest?*

- Rinse your mouth with water.

- Break off a small piece of the room-temperature chocolate and repeat the previous three steps with this piece. *Is the initial flavor of this chocolate stronger compared with the initial taste of the ice-cold chocolate? Does the flavor change as this piece melts?*

- Take more of the cold chocolate from the freezer, and compare the smell of the cold chocolate with that of the room-temperature chocolate. *Does one smell more strongly than the other? Could the difference in smell account for the difference in flavor?*

- Remove the ice cream from the freezer and scoop a small amount into a bowl.

- Compare the smell of the frozen ice cream with that of the room-temperature ice cream. *Which ice cream produces the strongest smell? Is there a perceivable difference?*

- Place a spoonful of frozen ice cream in your mouth. Close your mouth and concentrate on the flavor. *What is the flavor like? Is it too sweet, just right, or not sweet enough?*

- Let the ice cream melt in your mouth. *Does the flavor change as the ice cream melts? At what point do you experience the strongest flavor?*

- Rinse your mouth with water.

- Taste the room-temperature ice cream. *How is the flavor different from that of the frozen ice cream? Does it taste just as good? Why or why not?*

ExTRA

Ask volunteers to perform the same tests that you did. *Do they experience similar changes in perceived flavor as you did? Why do you think this happens?*

ExTRA

Taste more of the melted ice cream. Then, without rinsing your mouth, taste the frozen ice cream again. *Does the frozen ice cream taste as sweet as it did the first time you tasted it? Did eating something very sweet first change your perception of the next item you ate?*

19

EXTRA 〜〜〜〜〜〜〜〜

This activity compared ice-cold food with room-temperature food. Compare room-temperature milk or chocolate milk with warm versions. Be careful not to consume scorching-hot drinks! *Is the smell of one stronger than that of the other? Does one taste sweeter than the other?*

EXTRA 〜〜〜〜〜〜〜〜

This activity tests sweet food. Test if the same conclusions are valid for bitter or sour drinks or foods.

OBSERVATIONS AND RESULTS • • • • • • • • •

Did you notice the flavor of food changes as it undergoes a change in temperature?

Our sense of taste is more sensitive to warm food than to cold food. That is why the frozen ice cream probably tasted just sweet enough, whereas the melted version probably tasted much too sweet. Similarly, the frozen chocolate probably had very little taste until it warmed up in your mouth. The intensity of the taste increased as the food warmed up. The smell might have become stronger, but probably not drastically. If you tried the activity with food that had been heated, such as warm milk, you probably noticed that the intensity of the smell increased along with the intensity of the flavor.

Foods are prepared to be eaten at a certain temperature. When people prepare meals, they aim for the temperature the food will be served at that gives the desired flavor. In addition to flavor, however, people also think about the texture of food. So if the flavor of your pepperoni pizza is too strong, or if you want your ice cream to taste a little sweeter, cooling it or heating it might not be the ideal solution.

CLEANUP • • • • • • • • • • • • •

Wash the ice cream bowls and any other items that may have gotten dirty. Put other materials back where you found them.

⚛ Spot the Fat in Your Snack

WHAT'S IN YOUR SNACK? UNLEASH THE HIDDEN GREASE IN POTATO CHIPS TO FIND OUT. GRAPH THE FAT CONTENT TO SEE WHERE YOUR CHIPS FALL—AND DECIDE IF "LOW-FAT" CHIPS ARE ALL THAT THEY'RE CRACKED UP TO BE!

PROJECT TIME
🕐 25 to 30 minutes

KEY CONCEPTS
Fat
Nutrition
Food
Snacks

Do you enjoy eating potato chips? If you do, you are not alone. Potato chips are a very popular snack food. In fact, many people eat the equivalent of more than one bag of chips per month. When eating potato chips, have you ever noticed that your hands get greasy? Maybe you have heard people explaining that potato chips are bad for you because they contain too much fat—some of it unhealthful. Is this true? Try this activity and find out—by spotting the fat in potato chips!

21

BACKGROUND

Fats are actually a main component of our diet and are important for our bodies to work. A healthy diet consists of about 20 percent of calories from fat. Why is fat useful to us? Our body uses fat for storing energy and for digesting essential fat-soluble vitamins. Our brain also needs fats to function well. So why do we hear all these stories about bad fats? The reason is that there are different types of fats in foods and not all of them are healthy.

If you have ever looked at nutrition labels of foods, you might have noticed that the fat category is subdivided into "saturated," "unsaturated," and (sometimes) "trans" fats. The different names represent the various types of fats that result from each kind of fat molecule's chemical structure. But which of these are "bad" and which are "good" fats? Unsaturated fats—mostly found in plant-based foods and oils—have been shown to be beneficial to your health. Saturated fats—which mainly come from animal sources—have been associated with an increased risk of cardiovascular diseases. "Trans fats," in particular, which are artificially processed, should be avoided in a healthy diet.

Most food we eat has some amount of fat in it, often in an invisible form so we do not even notice it. But did you know that potato chips contain up to 35 percent fat? Some of this fat is greasy, meaning it is partly melted and leaves a film on many things it touches. Because of this, an easy way to make these fats visible is the grease spot test. Grab some chips and see for yourself in this activity!

MATERIALS

- Clean working area that can get greasy
- Graph paper
- Wax paper
- Two sheets of regular paper
- Rolling pin
- Scissors
- Timer
- Digital kitchen scale
- Two varieties of potato chips (Use regular chips and reduced-fat chips. It is best, but not required, if both varieties are the same brand.)
- Tape
- Well-lit window (and permission to tape pieces of paper to it)

PREPARATION

- With your scissors, carefully cut two pieces of graph paper into rectangles approximately 7 by 5 inches (18 by 13 cm).

- Cut two slightly larger size pieces of the wax paper.

- Take one sheet of the regular paper, the cut graph paper, and the wax paper and label each one "Regular Chips." Label the other set of three papers with "Reduced-Fat Chips."

- On the kitchen scale, weigh about 1 ounce (28 g) of each kind of potato chip, the regular and reduced-fat variety. Set each pile aside on your table for now.

PROCEDURE

- With your hands, take a couple of regular potato chips out of the bag. Look at them closely. *Do they look very greasy?*

- Crumble the potato chips with your fingers. *How do your fingers look? Can you see some shiny grease on them? How do your fingers feel when you rub them against one another?*

- After washing and thoroughly drying your hands, repeat the first and second steps with the reduced-fat chips. *Do they look very different? Are your hands less greasy after you crumble them with your fingers?*

- Clean your hands again and put the sheet of paper labeled "Regular Chips" down on the table. Take the piece of graph paper labeled "Regular Chips" and place it on top of the regular piece of paper.

- Take the pile of regular chips that you prepared and spread them evenly on the graph paper so the whole area is covered with chips.

- Place the wax paper labeled "Regular Chips" on top of the chips.

- Carefully press down on the wax paper and crush the chips. Try to keep the pieces evenly spread out on the graph paper. Use the rolling pin to crush the chips into smaller pieces.

- Set your timer for one minute, and let the crushed chips sit on the graph paper for the full minute. After the minute has passed, put the wax paper and the potato chips into the trash. Try to remove all of the extra chip bits from the graph paper, too. *Do you notice a grease stain on the graph paper? How large is the grease stain?*

- Tape the graph paper to a well-lit window so you can see the stain clearly; let it hang there for about 10 minutes. *How much of the graph paper is covered in grease? Are there any areas that are not translucent? What are the sizes of the individual grease stains on the graph paper?*

- Also look at the regular sheet of paper that was underneath the graph paper. *Did any of the grease spots leak through the graph paper? How many grease spots do you see on this sheet of paper?*

- Repeat steps 4 through 10 with the reduced-fat chips. *How does the grease spot on the graph paper look this time? Is more or less area of the graph paper covered with grease? What do you notice when you compare the sizes of the individual grease spots with the spots left by the regular chips? On the underlying sheet, do you count more or fewer grease spots?*

- Finally, look at the nutrition labels on both bags of potato chips. *How much fat is in each of them? Do these numbers agree with your grease spot results?*

EXTRA

As you look at the grease spots on the graph paper, try to count all the squares that are covered in grease; this way you also have a quantitative measurement of the fat content in the two different potato chip varieties. Compare the results for both of the chip varieties. *Did you expect these results? How many more squares were covered in grease using the regular chips compared with the reduced-fat ones?*

EXTRA

Often foods with reduced fats have additional ingredients to take the place of the missing fats. Examine the labels of the two bags of chips. *Do you see differences in the ingredient lists? What other differences do you see on the nutritional labels?*

⚛ SCIENCE FAIR IDEA

What other foods do you think contain a lot of invisible fats?
Try to produce grease spots with other foods that you find in your kitchen. Some examples of foods to try are nuts, chocolate, cheese, or cereals. *Were you surprised about any of your results?*

EXTRA

Potato chips are, of course, not the only type of "chip" you can eat as a snack. And many can easily be made at home—using healthier, unsaturated fats. With an adult, look online to find recipes for baked chips made from sweet potatoes, plantains, or even kale. *Could you make a snack that is healthier than store-bought potato chips?* With an adult's help, try out some of your new baked chip recipes!

OBSERVATIONS AND RESULTS · · · · · · · · ·

Did you see some really big grease spots on the graph paper after crushing the chips? This is no surprise—fat is a major ingredient in chips, as you probably noticed when you looked at their nutrition labels. When you just look at the chips, however, you do not necessarily see all the fat they contain. Only when you crumble the chips with your hands do you start to detect these invisible fats as your fingers become very shiny and slippery from all the grease.

In contrast to water, fats that get absorbed by paper cannot get enough heat to evaporate at room temperature. An easy way to test this is to take a sheet of paper and put one drop of oil next to a drop of water. At first, both areas look wet and translucent but after awhile the water evaporates and the spot dries whereas the fat spot remains visible. This is because when fat is absorbed into the paper's pores, the grease-stained part of the paper—which is normally white due to the scattering of light that shines through it—allows less scattering, and the light passes through it, appearing darker in color and translucent.

When you compared the two different potato chip varieties, you probably observed that most of the squares were covered with fat for the regular chips and the underlying sheet of paper might even have had significant grease stains as well. Using the reduced-fat chips, however, should have resulted in a much smaller grease-covered area, both on the graph paper as well as on the sheet underneath. This makes sense because these kinds of chips contain less fat that can be absorbed by the paper.

CLEANUP •

Throw away crushed chips and dirty paper.
Return other materials to where you found them.

Succulent Science
The Role of Fats in Making a Perfect Pastry

TEMPERATURE AND THE TYPE OF FAT YOU USE PLAY A BIG ROLE IN HOW PIECRUSTS TASTE AND FEEL. TRY THE FOLLOWING ACTIVITY TO SEE HOW YOU PREFER YOUR PIE!

Have you ever wanted to bake the perfect pie? No matter whether it is apple, chocolate, pecan, or pumpkin, every good pie needs a well-made piecrust. If the pastry crust is heavy or chewy, it can affect the taste of the whole pie. How do you make a pastry crust that is light and flaky? In this scrumptious science activity, you will find out by investigating how the temperature of fat used (in dough) can affect a pastry's texture and taste, all while baking your very own pastry crusts!

PROJECT TIME
1 1/2 to 2 hours

KEY CONCEPTS
Food science
Baking
Pastries
Fats

27

BACKGROUND

Going to a bakery can be a fun adventure—there is usually a display of delicious sweets and pastries to tempt the palate and the eyes. Many of these treats are made using wheat flour, which is an interesting substance. When you mix water with other powdery substances, the result is usually some sort of paste. But when you mix water with wheat flour, you get a very different material—one that is the base for so many tasty foods, such as breads, pastas, and pastries, including piecrusts. Crusts (also called pastry shells) were first developed in the Middle Ages to contain and preserve meat dishes, resulting in dishes such as the Cornish pasty.

The taste and texture of a pastry depends on the makeup of its dough, which typically contains water, flour, and fat. Gluten proteins in flour allow the dough to be plastic (it can change its shape) and elastic (it bounces back and returns to its original shape) and to turn into a fluffy baked product. The fat in the dough, on the other hand, helps give the final product its texture and flavor. Get ready to make homemade pastry crusts to find out how differently prepared fats affect them!

MATERIALS

- Ice water
- 1 cup of butter (Using butter in individually wrapped sticks makes it easy to measure the required amount.)
- Small pot
- Large mixing bowl
- Fork
- Measuring cups and spoons
- 3 cups of flour
- 1 teaspoon of kosher salt
- Pastry blender or two dinner knives
- Ruler
- Plastic wrap
- Timer, clock, or stopwatch
- Refrigerator
- Oven
- Large, hard cutting board
- Rolling pin
- Two aluminum pie pans, each 9 inches (23 cm) in diameter
- Oven mitts
- Hot pad
- Volunteers (at least three, to do some pastry shell tasting!)

PREPARATION

- Wash your hands, make sure all of your cooking equipment is clean, and check that your ingredients are out and ready to use.

- Prepare ice water by filling a small bowl with ice cubes and then adding cold water until the bowl is nearly full. Add fresh ice cubes as they melt.

- Right before you're ready to start, begin melting 1/2 cup of butter in a small pot on the stove, on low heat. Keep the butter warm and melted until you are ready to use it. Use adult assistance and supervision when using the stove and oven and when handling hot items.

PROCEDURE

- Measure 1 1/3 cups of flour and place it into the large mixing bowl. Measure 1/2 teaspoon of kosher salt and mix it completely into the flour with the fork.

- Add 1/2 cup of cold, refrigerated butter to the flour mixture and use the pastry blender to work the butter into the flour. If you do not have access to a pastry blender, use two dinner knives to "cut" the butter into the flour. (Ask an adult before you use knives in this activity.) Blend or cut the butter into the flour for approximately seven to 10 minutes. The result should be small, pea-size (or smaller) pieces of fat-coated flour. *How hard is it to mix the cold butter with the flour?*

- Once the flour mixture is the right texture, add 3 tablespoons (44 ml) of ice water to the bowl. Use the fork to blend the water into the flour mixture. *How easily does the water blend in?*

- Once the water is completely blended into the flour mixture, quickly gather the dough into a ball and flatten it into a 4-inch (10 cm) wide disk with your hands. *How well does the dough collect into a ball?*

29

- Wrap the dough with a piece of plastic wrap and put it into the refrigerator for 20 minutes. At the same time, preheat the oven to 425°F (218°C).

- While the first batch of dough is in the refrigerator, prepare a second batch, but this time, use the melted butter you prepared. Again, measure and mix together 1 1/3 cups of flour and 1/4 teaspoon of kosher salt. Then blend in the 1/2 cup of melted butter. *How hard is it to mix the melted butter with the flour?*

- After the butter is mixed in, blend in 3 tablespoons (44 ml) of ice water, collect the dough into a ball and flatten it into a 4-inch (10 cm) wide disk. *How easy was it to blend in the water and collect the dough into a ball this time?*

- Wrap the dough with a piece of plastic wrap and put it in the refrigerator for 20 minutes.

- When the first batch of dough is ready, lightly flour the rolling pin and the large, hard cutting board. Roll the dough disk from the center out, in each direction, forming approximately a 12-inch (30.5 cm) circle. *How easy is it to make the circle?*

- Transfer the dough to the 9-inch (23 cm) pie pan. To do this, a trick you can use is to flip the pie pan upside down and place it on top of the rolled-out dough. Then carefully flip the dough and pie pan over (by putting your hand underneath the cutting board) so that the dough now lies on top of the pie pan.

- Gently press the dough against the bottom and sides of the pie pan. Trim any dough that is hanging over the edge of the pie pan with a knife. Prick the bottom and sides of the dough with a fork.

- Bake the pastry shell for 15 to 18 minutes at 425°F (218°C).

- While the first batch of dough is baking, you can prepare the second batch after it is done refrigerating. Prepare it as you did the first batch (using the other pie pan). *How easy is it to roll this dough into a 12-inch (30.5 cm) circle?*

- Once you have prepared the pastry shell using the second batch of dough, also bake it for 15 to 18 minutes at 425°F (218°C).

- When each pastry shell is done baking, carefully remove it from the oven (using oven mitts). Place each pie pan on a hot pad to let it cool. The pastry shells should be golden brown. *How does each baked pastry shell look compared with one another? How are they similar? How are they different?*

- Once the pastry shells have cooled, gather your volunteers and have them look at and taste pieces of each shell. *Which pastry shell is the flakiest? Which is most tender?* (You can define tenderness as how easy it is to chew a piece of the shell or how soft it is in your mouth when you chew it.)

- *How do you think the type of butter (melted or refrigerated) used affected how the pastry shells turned out?*

ExTRA

Repeat this activity, but skip the step where you chill the dough in the refrigerator. *Is chilling the dough required to make a good pastry shell?*

ExTRA

Try this recipe using lard and/or vegetable shortening instead of butter. *Does using one of these other ingredients make a good pastry shell? How do pastry shells made with these different types of fats compare?*

ExTRA

If you have access to a microscope, you could do a closer inspection of the piecrusts. *How do the piecrusts compare with one another when they are viewed through a microscope?*

OBSERVATIONS AND RESULTS ··········

Did you and your volunteers find the pastry shell made using refrigerated butter to be bumpier, less tender, and flakier than the pastry shell made using melted butter?

When mixing the butter into the pastry shell dough, you probably found it much harder to mix in the cold butter (which was solid and difficult to break into pieces) than to mix in the melted butter (which was liquid and so should have easily blended with the flour, salt, and ice water). When rolling out the chilled disk of dough, you should have similarly found it much easier to roll out the dough with the melted butter than the dough made with the cold butter. Overall, the melted butter should have more easily coated and separated the flour particles from one another, which resulted in a smoother pastry shell. You and your volunteers may have also generally found the pastry shell made using melted butter to be less flaky and more tender than the pastry shell made using cold butter, although some people may differ in their opinions.

CLEANUP ··············

Wash your utensils and dishes and enjoy snacking on the remaining piecrusts!

Scrumptious Science
Shaking Up Butter

EASILY MAKE YOUR VERY OWN BUTTER FROM SCRATCH WITH THE FOLLOWING ACTIVITY!

Have you ever wondered how butter is made? How does that creamy spread come from something as liquid as cow's milk? Making butter by hand can be hard work, but it can be easily made at home! In this activity, you'll not only get to find out how butter is made, but also how temperature affects the butter-making process. And then you may enjoy the fruits (or rather, toppings) of your labors!

PROJECT TIME
30 minutes, plus 5 hours of preparation time

KEY CONCEPTS
Food science
Chemistry
Fat
Heat

33

BACKGROUND

Butter is an ancient prepared food, having been made by people at least 4,000 years ago. Some of the earliest known recipes for making butter call for the use of a container made from animal skin. The skin would be sewed together tightly, leaving a small opening through which to add fatty milk or cream. The vessel would then be suspended, such as from wooden poles, and swung until butter formed. For the last century, however, most butter has been produced in factories.

One traditional butter-making process begins with making cream. When whole milk sits out, tiny fat molecules float to the top, forming a layer of cream that can be skimmed and collected. To make butter, the cream is agitated (stirred up) so that the fat molecules get shaken out of position and clump together. Eventually, after enough agitation, the fat molecules clump so much that butter forms. When this happens, the fat molecules have clearly separated from the liquid in the cream, and this liquid can be removed and made into buttermilk.

MATERIALS

- Measuring cup
- 1 cup (237 ml) of heavy whipping cream
- Cup or glass
- One clean 1-quart (946 ml) glass jar with lid and a tight seal. A canning jar with a lid, seal, and ring works best. A different size jar could be used, but the amount of heavy whipping cream should be adjusted accordingly.
- Helper (optional)
- Stopwatch or clock
- Bowl
- Cold water
- Small plastic bags

PREPARATION

- Pour 1/2 cup (118 ml) of heavy whipping cream into a cup or glass. Let it sit out at room temperature for about 5 hours.

PROCEDURE

- After the 1/2 cup (118 ml) of heavy whipping cream has sat out for 5 hours, pour it into a clean 1-quart (946 ml) glass jar. Put the lid on the jar and screw it on tightly.

- For the next step, you may want to get a helper ready to trade off on shaking the jar. It will take several minutes of vigorous shaking to make butter from the cream!

- When you start shaking the jar, start the stopwatch or note what time it is. *How does the heavy whipping cream change as you shake the jar?* As the cream thickens (within a couple of minutes of when you start shaking), keep shaking the jar!

- Shake the jar until butter forms. This could take between 5 to 20 minutes. Once you have shaken the jar enough, the liquid will suddenly separate from the butter. The butter will be a pale yellow lump, and the liquid will be milky. You'll probably hear the lump hitting the sides of the jar as you shake it. When the butter and liquid separate, stop shaking the jar and stop the stopwatch.

- *How long did it take the butter to form when using room-temperature cream? How do the butter and liquid in the jar look?*

- Carefully pour the liquid out of the jar. You can store the liquid and use it as buttermilk for other recipes.

- Remove the lump of butter from the jar and place it in a bowl of cold water. Gently knead the butter to remove any extra liquid. Use your fingers to drain the liquid from the bowl. Rinse the butter two more times in this way. (If the liquid is not removed, the butter will go rancid faster.)

- Transfer the butter into a small plastic bag and store it.

- Clean the jar, its lid, and the bowl.

- Repeat the entire butter-making process as you just did, but this time use 1/2 cup (118 ml) of cold heavy whipping cream straight from the refrigerator (instead of room-temperature heavy whipping cream). Try to shake the jar similarly. *How long did it take the butter to form when using the colder cream? How do the butter and liquid in the jar look?*

- *Overall, how long did it take butter to form using the warmer heavy whipping cream compared with the colder cream? Does it look like the temperature affects how quickly the cream turns into butter?*

ExTRA

Repeat this activity a few more times. *Do you get similar results each time you use refrigerated heavy whipping cream and each time you use room-temperature cream, or is there variation in your results?*

ExTRA

Weigh the amount of heavy whipping cream that you start with and then weigh the amount of butter that you end with. *How much of the cream turned into butter?*

 ## SCIENCE FAIR IDEA

In this activity, you investigated how temperature affects turning heavy whipping cream into butter, but you did not quantify the temperatures you used. You could repeat this activity, but this time use a thermometer to measure the temperature of the cream when you put it into the glass jar. You could even try some different temperatures of cream and see how that affects the process. *How do different temperatures of cream affect the butter-making process?*

OBSERVATIONS AND RESULTS ··········

Did it take a much longer amount of time to make butter using the chilled heavy whipping cream compared with using the room-temperature heavy whipping cream? Aside from this difference, did both butters seem similar?

As you shook each jar, you should have seen and heard the cream initially slosh around, and then gradually the sloshing slowed as the cream thickened. Eventually, after several seconds (but less than two minutes), it should have become so thick that it didn't move much as you shook the jar. At this point, the cream had likely turned into whipped cream. After you shook the jar for about 5 to 20 minutes total, the cream should have abruptly turned into butter. This likely happened much quicker for the room-temperature cream than for the colder cream. (For example, the room-temperature cream may have become butter after 5 to 6 minutes, whereas the refrigerated cream took 13 to 15 minutes of shaking.) As the cream is shaken, the fat molecules get out of position and clump together, eventually clumping so much that butter forms. At this point, the fat molecules have clearly separated from the liquid in the cream. When molecules are heated, they move faster because they have more energy. Consequently, the molecules in the room-temperature cream moved faster than the ones in the chilled cream, allowing the room-temperature fat molecules to clump together faster, thereby forming butter faster.

CLEANUP ·················

You may enjoy some delicious, homemade butter. Be sure to keep it refrigerated and consume it before it becomes rancid.

Food Sleuthing
Find the Missing Ingredient

CAN YOU FIND THE MISSING INGREDIENT? LEARN ABOUT NUTRITION LABELING AND SEE IF YOU DEDUCE WHAT MIGHT BE LEFT OUT.

PROJECT TIME
20 to 30 minutes

KEY CONCEPTS
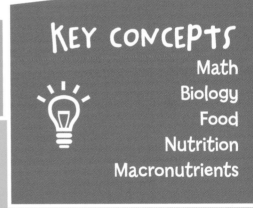
Math
Biology
Food
Nutrition
Macronutrients

Food ads and labels bombard us with enticing slogans and attractive images, luring us into consuming a certain food. But have you ever wondered how nutritious an advertised food is? Have you ever examined a nutrition facts label and wondered what the columns of words and numbers really meant? This activity will shed some light on the label. You will explore serving sizes and nutrients—and might find a discrepancy. Why would the sum of the nutrients not always add up to the total? Like a detective, you will gather the facts, brainstorm ideas, and find evidence to support your proposed explanation. Can you crack the case?

38

BACKGROUND

Food laws and regulations have been around for centuries. Their initial goal was to deter misbranding food, such as labeling and selling honey diluted with cheap corn syrup as pure honey. The mandatory U.S. nutrition facts label that we know today is a result of the 1990 Nutrition Labeling and Education Act. It informs consumers about what is in their food by listing serving size (the amount of food usually consumed at one time) and basic per-serving nutritional information including calorie (energy) content, essential vitamins and minerals, and recommended daily amounts of key nutrients. All of this information can be used to make informed decisions when deciding what to eat.

Foods mainly consist of fat, carbohydrates, and protein. These are called macronutrients.

• Fats can enhance flavor and texture. Health experts advise you to avoid saturated and trans fats. That said, some fats, especially unsaturated fats, are an essential part of a healthy diet. As an example, they support healthy nerve and brain function.

• Carbohydrates are the sugars, starches, and dietary fiber in our foods. Sugars and starches provide us with energy; fiber promotes healthy bowel function.

• Proteins are needed to build and repair the body. They are an essential part of a healthy diet, but consuming too much protein can damage the kidneys.

The other nutrients listed, such as vitamin A, iron, calcium, etc., are called micronutrients. Although they are present in much smaller amounts, they play an important role in a healthy diet. For easy reference, the labels show the percent daily value for most nutrients. This refers to the portion of the daily recommendations for this nutrient one serving provides.

MATERIALS

- Nutrition facts labels from a:
  • dry food item, such as bread, crackers, etc.
  • nut butter or dairy butter
  • moist food item, such as yogurt, canned fruit or vegetables, etc.
  • water bottle
- Additional nutrition facts labels (optional)
- Calculator (optional)

PREPARATION

- Gather all of your nutrition facts labels in one place. *What do you think you might discover by comparing the foods you have selected?*

PROCEDURE

- Read the nutrition facts label of a dry food item such as bread or crackers. *Can you find the mass of one serving of this food item?* This will probably be measured in grams or ounces. (One ounce is about 28 grams.)

- Skip the calorie information and go straight to the list of macronutrients: Total Fat, Total Carbohydrates, and Protein. These are the nutrients that make up the bulk of our food.

- Fats often enhance flavor and texture. Consuming them in limited amounts is essential for health. *Can you find the mass (in grams) of fat one serving of this food contains?*

- Jump to the Total Carbohydrates. Carbohydrates are mainly found in plant-based foods like grains, fruits, and vegetables. Our bodies break these down into sugar that provides us with energy or into fiber that keeps our bowels healthy. *Can you find the mass (in grams) of carbohydrates in one serving of this food?*

- Find the last macronutrient, Protein. Your body needs protein to grow and repair essential parts like muscles, bones, and blood. *Can you find the mass (in grams) of protein in one serving of this food?*

- Check if it all adds up. *If you add the masses of fat, carbohydrates, and protein in one serving, is this sum (almost) identical to the mass of one serving of this food? Why do you think this is the case?*

- **Note:** Other nutrients such as sodium (salt) might be listed as well. Their mass per serving is usually expressed in milligrams (mg). There are 1,000 milligrams in a gram, so although these nutrients are important for a healthy diet, they do not add much mass to a serving of food.

- Look for a nutrition facts label of nut or dairy butter. *Can you find the mass of one serving of butter?*

- Next, look for the total masses of fat, carbohydrates, and protein contained in a serving and add them up. *Is the sum (almost) identical to the mass of one serving of this food?*

- Look for a label of yogurt or canned fruit or vegetables and repeat the previous step. *Are you surprised about the result?*

- Analyze a few more nutrition labels from different types of food. *What do you notice? Does the sum of the masses of macronutrients (fats, carbohydrates, and protein) in a serving match the total mass of a serving in some cases and not in others? Why would that be?*

- Group the foods where the sum is close. *Do these food items have anything in common?* Make a second group where the sum does not match. *Do these food items have anything in common? Could there be something missing on the label that is absent in the first group but present in the second?*

- Get into a detective mode. *Can you see a pattern? Can you come up with an explanation for what you noticed? Which cases support your explanation? Can you think of other food items that, when analyzed, could provide evidence for or against your explanation?*

- Look at the nutrition label of a water bottle. The serving size will probably be expressed in milliliters (ml) or ounces (oz). *Can you analyze this label, knowing that one milliliter of water weighs one gram? How does the sum of the masses of macronutrients in a serving of water match up with the total mass of a serving of water? Does this support or refute your explanation?*

41

EXTRA

Group foods that provide either lots of fats, carbohydrates, or protein. *Do some foods belong in two or even all three groups? Do some foods belong in none of them?*

EXTRA

Rank your foods from smallest to largest serving sizes. *Are you surprised about the variety in serving sizes?*

EXTRA

Pick a food item you eat frequently and weigh out one serving as listed on the label. *Is what you usually eat more, less, or about the same as the serving size? Repeat for other food items. Do you observe a pattern in the mismatches in serving size and what you usually eat?*

EXTRA

Nutrition facts labels list nutritional content per serving. *Can you calculate nutritional content per 100 grams instead?* For example, divide the amount of fats per serving (in grams) by the serving size (in grams). This will give you the amount of fats per gram of the food. Multiply this by 100 to get the amount per 100 grams of food. Now rank your foods from highest to lowest fats per 100 grams. *How does this ranking compare with ranking by fats per serving? Which ranking would be more useful for consumers who are looking for food high (or low) in fats?* Repeat for carbohydrates and protein.

OBSERVATIONS AND RESULTS ·········

Did you notice that for some food items, the sum of the masses of macronutrients (fats, carbohydrates, and protein) in a serving is very close to the mass of one serving whereas for others it is not? This occurs because water has mass but contains no macronutrients.

Although consuming enough water is essential, it is not listed on the nutrition facts label. Thus, the water content of food influences its mass, but not its nutritional content. Foods containing water will have servings that weigh more than the sum of the masses per serving of the three macronutrients. The mass discrepancies you observed informed you about the water content of the food items. The more water they contained, the bigger the discrepancy.

Listing nutritional content per serving allows consumers to compare different types of food at a glance and identify which provides more of a nutrient per serving. Pay attention to serving sizes though! You might find that you usually consume way more or way less than the listed serving size, making these comparisons a little trickier.

CLEANUP ··················
Return the materials to where you found them.

Cucumber Chemistry
Moisture Capture with Desiccants

CAN YOU SHRINK A CUCUMBER SLICE WITH JUST A LITTLE BIT OF SALT, SUGAR, OR BAKING POWDER?

PROJECT TIME
45 to 60 minutes

KEY CONCEPTS
Material science
Food science
Chemistry
Water absorption

Have you ever gotten an electronic gadget wet and had it stop working? It would be great if you could somehow dry it out before the internal parts got damaged, right? There are actually some substances that can absorb water from their surroundings. You might have noticed when you buy new shoes, electronics, or beef jerky that often there is a little package inside with the warning: "silica gel, do not eat." This little bag of gel protects the product from minor water damage, such as when it is very humid. Imagine your jerky all moist and slimy—it wouldn't have the texture you were expecting! In this fun activity, you will use a cucumber to explore how different substances can absorb water from their environments. You may be surprised how the cucumber will change when exposed to salt, sugar, or baking powder. And you will discover how you might be able to rescue an electronic gadget the next time it gets wet!

44

BACKGROUND

Some materials or substances can attract water from their surrounding environment—they are called hygroscopic. The water molecules they absorb can either be trapped in pores of the material, weakly bonded with molecules of the substance, or can form "water of crystallization," which is water that occurs inside a crystal structure of compounds such as salt. Some compounds even absorb so much water that they dissolve into a liquid solution. These materials are called deliquescent.

But what is all this useful for? Actually, hygroscopic materials are all around you. Some common ones include wood, clay, and wool. Because hygroscopic substances do such a good job of absorbing water, they are often used as drying agents or desiccants, like the little silica gel packages. Those are helpful when you want to keep a product very dry. To determine how hygroscopic a material is, scientists measure how much water it absorbs, depending on the relative humidity of the environment. And now you can test some of these impressive materials right at home. Let's get started and explore what substances in your kitchen can absorb water from their surroundings.

MATERIALS

- Cucumber
- Sugar
- Baking powder
- Salt
- Kitchen scale (optional)
- Knife (and adult help using it)
- Four small plates
- Teaspoon
- Watch or clock
- Flat workspace large enough to set up all of your materials

PREPARATION

- Take the unpeeled cucumber and, with the help of an adult, cut four equal-sized pieces with a knife. The slices should be about 0.2 inch (0.5 cm) thick. *What does the cucumber slice look like? Is it very wet? How does it feel when you touch it? Does it feel crisp, hard, or squishy? When you pick it up, does it keep its stiffness?*

- If you have a kitchen scale, you can weigh each of the cucumber slices and write down the weight of each slice.

- Put each slice on a different plate; each slice will now get a different treatment.

PROCEDURE

- Measure out 1 teaspoon of salt. Feel the salt. *Is it very dry?* For the first slice, carefully pour the salt on top of the cucumber slice. The salt should not fall off the cucumber but rather form a little pile on top. *What do you think will happen to the salt or cucumber?*

- Measure out 1 teaspoon of sugar. Touch the sugar with your fingers. *How does it feel?* Now build a little pile with the sugar on top of the second cucumber slice. *Do you think the sugar will feel or look different after awhile?*

- Measure out 1 teaspoon of baking powder. *How does it look and feel?* Pile the baking powder on top of the third cucumber slice. *What do you think might happen in this case?*

- Cucumber slice four will be your control, meaning it receives no treatment and is the one against which you will compare your results. You leave it on the plate as it is.

- Observe all four cucumber slices for 30 minutes. Watch closely what happens to the different substances you have put on each slice. You can also use the teaspoon to gently press the pile onto the cucumber occasionally. (Be sure to clean the teaspoon between touching it to each substance.) *Do you notice any texture change of the different substances? What happens to them over time?*

- During the same 30 minutes, touch the salt, sugar, and baking powder every five minutes with your fingers. (Be sure you rinse your fingers off between each.) *How do they feel? Do they start to change over time?*

- If the substances become wet, take a clean spoon and carefully remove the pile of sugar, salt, or baking powder and replace it with the same amount of fresh sugar, salt, or baking powder. Make a note of how often you changed the pile for each substance. *Which of the substances became wet first? How often do you think you will have to replace the salt, sugar, or baking powder?*

- After 30 minutes, remove all the sugar, salt, and baking soda from the cucumbers (keeping track of which slice had which substance on in). Use your fingers to clean the cucumber slices of any remaining substance. *When touching the different cucumber slices, how do they feel? Do they feel different? Do some still feel crisp or did they become squishy?*

- Once all your cucumber slices are clean, if you have a kitchen scale, you can weigh each cucumber slice and note any changes. Compare this value with the number you wrote down in the beginning. *What happened to the cucumber slice during the activity? Did it become heavier or lighter? Comparing the different substances, which one resulted in the biggest change? Can you think of a reason why?*

- Finally, cut your cucumber slices in half and compare the texture and thickness of each slice with that of your control. *Did their texture and appearance change? If yes, how? Did the slice thickness change? Which substance had the most noticeable effect? What does that tell you about the substance's ability to attract water?*

⚛ SCIENCE FAIR IDEA

You have tested salt, sugar, and baking soda in this activity. *Now, can you think of other substances to try that might be hygroscopic?*

During your test of some of these substances, the cucumber lost a lot of water. *Do you think you could rehydrate the cucumber again?* After your dehydration test, try placing each cucumber slice into a clean cup of fresh water and let it sit overnight. *Do the cucumber slices look different in the morning?*

OBSERVATIONS AND RESULTS ·········

Did you observe the cucumber slices shrinking? The fresh cucumber should have remained very crisp and moist over the 30 minutes you observed it. This is because 96 percent of a cucumber is actually water. For the slices with salt, sugar, or baking powder on top, you should have noticed that over time the substances became wet and soaked up the water from the cucumber. You probably had to exchange the salt most often throughout the activity. After 30 minutes, the experimental cucumber slices should have lost some weight. The slices may have become thinner and much squishier compared with the control slice. Some of these slices might actually have begun to even look smaller.

There are several reasons for the cucumber shrinking. One is the hygroscopic property of the substances you tested. Salt has a strong ability to absorb water from its surroundings. Above a relative humidity of about 75 percent, salt will even become deliquescent, meaning it takes up so much water that it becomes a solution. Sugar is also hygroscopic; it forms weak bonds with the water molecules in its surroundings. In fact, this property is very useful when baking cakes and cookies. Have you ever noticed that a crispy cookie becomes chewy after it is left out for awhile? This is because sugar absorbs water from the air, which makes the cookie moist. Although baking soda is less hygroscopic, your cucumber slice with baking soda on it might still have lost some weight, which means that the baking powder is able to absorb some water from the cucumber.

Besides hygroscopy, osmosis also contributes to the observed water loss in the cucumber. The water inside the cucumber does not contain much salt or sugar, but water on top of the slice will have a high concentration of salt or sugar. To compensate for this imbalance, the water inside the cucumber cells starts moving through the cell membranes into the high concentrations of salt or sugar water on top; this process is called osmosis. It is also the reason why you get so thirsty after eating lots of salty and sweet food. The high amount of salt or sugar in the food "pulls out" the water in your cells, which leads to the brain telling you to drink more water.

Now we come back to the beginning: How can hygroscopy help your electronic gadget? The next time a device gets wet, once you have turned it off and dried it from the outside, try putting it in an airtight baggie and add a very hygroscopic substance. The hygroscopic powers of salt-filled teabags or those little silica gel packages might just do the trick to dry it out and get it working again.

CLEANUP

If you compost, you can compost your cucumber slices. Otherwise, the cucumber slices, salt, sugar, and baking powder can be disposed of in the trash.

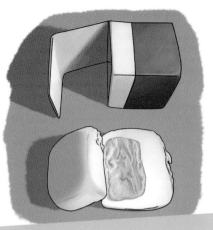

⚛ Shape-Shifting Science
Molding Hard-Boiled Eggs

ALL EGGS ARE ROUND—RIGHT? TRY THE FOLLOWING ACTIVITY TO SEE IF YOU CAN USE SCIENCE TO MOLD A HARD-BOILED EGG INTO DIFFERENT SHAPES!

PROJECT TIME
🕐 60 to 75 minutes

KEY CONCEPTS
Food science
Chemistry
Protein
Cooking

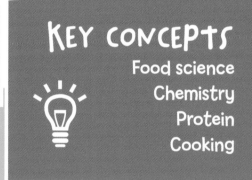

When it comes to food, presentation matters. Creativity and science, combined, can result in fascinating ways to cook and present food; hard-boiled eggs are just one example. Some interesting chemistry happens when you cook an egg. For example, think about how an egg starts out as a thick, liquid, translucent substance. But after heating the egg, it turns into a gel-like substance, which after further heating and cooling turns into a rubbery solid. How do the egg white and the yolk change during this process? When exactly does the egg turn hard? In this science activity, you will explore the flexibility of hard-boiled eggs, creating a delicious, fun-shaped reward!

BACKGROUND

Egg white is mainly made up of water (about 85 percent) and protein molecules (about 10 percent). The proteins are twisted, folded, and curled up like tiny, entangled balls of yarn floating around in the water. Heating causes the weak chemical bonds that keep these proteins entangled to break. The egg proteins then unravel and bump into other uncurled proteins, causing them to bond to one another, a process called coagulation. Water molecules are now trapped in a network of interconnected proteins. The egg white takes on a gel-like consistency, becoming a flexible solid. While the egg is still hot, the protein bonds can be molded into different shapes. Additional bonds between the proteins form until the egg cools. The longer the egg is left at a high temperature, the more protein bonds form, and the more rubbery the final egg will be. Once the egg has cooled down completely, however, the shape of the egg becomes permanent.

MATERIALS

- Plastic square box, 1.5 inches (3.8 cm) wide by 1.5 inches (3.8 cm) long and 1.5 inches (3.8 cm) high. If you do not have one available, you can make one from an empty quarter-gallon (or larger) milk or juice carton, tape, and scissors. (Use caution and an adult's help when cutting the carton).
- Rubber band long enough to go around the square box
- Cooking oil or spray
- Two extra-large eggs (Less-fresh eggs will peel more easily.)
- Saucepan
- Water
- Stove (Use caution and an adult's help when using the stove and handling hot items in this activity.)
- Timer
- Slotted or regular spoon
- Plate
- Paper towels or kitchen towel
- Oven mitt
- Kitchen knife

PREPARATION

- If you do not have a plastic square box measuring 1.5 inches (3.8 cm) on each side available, make one from an empty juice or milk carton. Here are the steps: First, clean out the empty carton, then cut it open so it lies flat. Draw the template of an open folded cubical box on the carton (making sure you draw an attached lid as well) with sides with dimensions of 1.5 inches (3.8 cm) in width, height, and length. Cut out the template, fold it into a box, and bind it together with tape, leaving one side open as a lid.

- Grease the inside of your square box with oil.

PROCEDURE

- Place two eggs in the saucepan. Add enough water so there is 0.5 inch (1.3 cm) covering the eggs. Put the saucepan on the stove.

- Heat the water until it comes to a rapid boil and keep it boiling for 10 minutes. *How do you think the contents of the egg are changing during this time?*

- Turn off the heat.

- Use the slotted spoon to take one egg out of the water and carefully place it on a plate where it can cool completely.

- Use the slotted spoon to take the second egg out of the saucepan. Do not discard the hot water; you will need it to keep the egg warm.

- Place this egg on several paper towels or a kitchen towel and carefully wrap the towel(s) around the egg. Use an oven mitt to protect your hand while you handle the hot egg.

- Gently tap the wrapped egg against the plate to crack the shell all over. Unwrap the egg and carefully peel away the shell. *What consistency does the cooked egg have?*

- Place the egg back on the spoon to dip it back into the hot water to wash away small pieces of shell. This also helps keep the egg hot.

- Gently push the hot egg that has had its shell removed pointed end first into the box without breaking the egg. *How does the egg feel? Is it wobbly, gel-like, rubbery, or stiff? Is it possible to fit the egg completely into the box?*

- The egg should just fill the box. If the egg does not completely fill the box, add some folded paper towels on top of your egg to fill the box completely.

- Put the lid on the box and put a rubber band around it to keep the box closed.

- Let both eggs—the unpeeled and the boxed egg—cool down for at least 30 minutes. Placing both eggs in the refrigerator can speed up the process.

- Once the eggs are cool, open the box and let that egg slide out on the plate. *How does the egg look? What is its shape? Touch it; does the egg feel differently than when it was hot?*

- Carefully peel the unpeeled egg by gently tapping it on the plate to crack its shell all over, then peel away the shell.

- Gently push this egg, pointed end first, into the box. *How does the egg feel? Is it wobbly, gel-like, rubbery, or stiff? Is it possible to squeeze the egg into the box without damaging it?*

- Now that you have successfully molded the other egg into a cube, cut the cubed egg open with a knife to make some more observations. *What shape is the egg yolk of the cubed egg? Is it any different from the egg yolk in hard-boiled eggs you have seen before?*

- *Are you curious if a cubed egg tastes any different?* This is your chance to try it out!

SCIENCE FAIR IDEA

You just cubed an egg! *Could you mold an egg in other forms, such as a pyramid, cylinder, or ball?* Use an empty juice box or milk carton to create other molds. Cookie cutters placed between two flat objects can lead to molds for even more shapes. *Any ideas on what the constraints on the dimensions of an egg mold will be? Should it have a particular volume? How flat would you be able to mold an egg?*

EXTRA

Try creating an egg mold with your hands. Let cold water run briefly over the egg as you hold it to cool it down abruptly. *Does an egg instantly keep its form after abrupt chilling or does it need long, slow cooling to make the form permanent?*

 ## SCIENCE FAIR IDEA

Experiment with different boiling times. *Can you mold a soft-boiled egg? How long do you need to keep the egg at a high temperature for it to keep its new form?*

OBSERVATIONS AND RESULTS · · · · · · · · ·

Did you successfully mold the egg while it was still hot? Were you unable to force the cold hard-boiled egg into the cube without breaking it?

While hot, the egg should have felt like a wobbly, gel-like flexible solid. This is because bonds between proteins are still being formed. While hot, these bonds can be manipulated so the hot egg can be squeezed into a cube without breaking. As the egg cooled in the box, more protein bonds were formed, giving the egg white a more rubbery character. Once cold, however, the protein bonds were permanently set, like a solid, so it kept its cube form after you slid the egg out of the box.

The other hard-boiled egg cooled down with its eggshell as its mold. Once cool, it kept the permanent egg shape we are so used to. It felt stiff, and because the protein bonds were set permanently it was impossible to squeeze the cold hard-boiled egg into the cube without breaking it.

After cutting the egg open, you should have seen the shape of the egg yolk changed as well. The egg yolk of the cubed egg should have been cubed and the egg yolk of the egg that cooled in its shell should have remained spherical.

You can mold eggs into other geometric forms as long as the volume is that of the egg used. This is because the hot hard-boiled egg has a fixed volume, but not a fixed form; the cold hard-boiled egg has a fixed volume and a fixed form.

CLEANUP · · · · · · · · · · · · · ·

If you haven't already, you can eat your boiled eggs or put them in the trash—and either way, you can compost the shells.

Solidifying Science
Why Can Certain Fruits Ruin Your Gelatin Dessert?

MAKE SURE YOUR GELATIN TREAT STAYS WIGGLY WITH THE FOLLOWING ACTIVITY.

Have you ever noticed that if you're making a gelatin dessert, such as JELL-O, it's not recommended to use certain fruits, like pineapple? Why is this? These fruits may prevent the gelatin from solidifying. In this activity, you'll get to determine if certain enzymes in some fruits can keep the gelatin from gelling—and whether there's a way to still include these fruits without ruining your gelatin dessert!

PROJECT TIME
30 minutes, plus up to 4 hours of waiting time

KEY CONCEPTS
Food science
Chemistry
Gelatin
Fruits
Enzymes
Heat

BACKGROUND ●

If you like making gelatin for dessert, the box often recommends not adding certain kinds of fruit, including pineapple, kiwi, mango, papaya, figs, or guava. People have a hard time getting the gelatin to solidify when they add these fruits. Gelatin is made from collagen, which is a structural protein found in all animals. Collagen is found in many parts of the body and helps give animals their structure, or shape. Gelatin, which is a mixture of collagen proteins, solidifies when you cook it because its proteins form tangled mesh pockets that trap the water and other ingredients. After the gelatin cools, the proteins remained tangled. This results in your wiggly-jiggly gelatin dessert.

The fruits listed above contain proteases, which are enzymes. Enzymes help make certain chemical reactions happen. Proteases specifically act like a pair of scissors, helping reactions take place that cut other proteins up. In this activity, you'll explore whether these protease enzymes are preventing the gelatin from solidifying (by cutting the gelatin's collagen proteins into such small pieces that they are no longer able to tangle together and create a semisolid structure). To do this, you'll inactivate these proteases by using heat.

MATERIALS 〜〜〜〜〜〜〜〜〜〜〜〜〜〜〜〜〜

- 1 cup of one of the following types of fruit, which should contain proteases: figs, guava, kiwi fruit, mango, papaya, or pineapple. Make sure the fruit is fresh.
- Knife
- Cutting board
- Measuring cup
- Water
- Stove top
- Fruit/vegetable steamer (optional)
- Pot, large enough to hold 3 cups (710 ml) of liquid
- Clock
- Three plastic cups or drinking glasses, each at least 12 ounces (355 ml) in size
- Tape and permanent marker or pen (optional)
- Gelatin mix (such as JELL-O), enough to make 3 cups of gelatin
- Three utensils for stirring, such as spoons or forks
- Refrigerator

PREPARATION

- You may want to have an adult help cut up the fruit and use the stove.

- Carefully cut up 1 cup of the fresh fruit.

- Cook 1/2 cup of the cut fruit. Do this by either steaming or boiling the fruit (with about 1/4 cup [59 ml] of water) for five minutes. *How does the cooked fruit look?*

- Add the raw fruit to one plastic cup or drinking glass and the cooked fruit to a different plastic cup. If it's difficult to tell the difference between the raw and cooked fruit by looking at them, you may want to label the cups (with tape and a permanent marker or pen).

PROCEDURE

- Make the gelatin dessert according to the package instructions. You will want to prepare at least 3 cups (710 ml) of liquid gelatin.

- Add 1 cup (237 ml) of gelatin liquid to each of the cups with fruit, and add the third cup portion to an empty cup. You should now have three cups with gelatin liquid in them.

- Thoroughly stir the contents of each cup. Use a different, clean utensil to stir each cup.

- Refrigerate all three cups, noting the time at which you put them inside the refrigerator.

- An hour after you put the cups in the refrigerator, check the consistency of the gelatin. Continue checking their consistency once an hour until the gelatin in the cup without fruit solidifies. (This will probably take about four hours.) *In which condition(s) does the gelatin set? In which condition(s) does the gelatin remain a liquid? Are there any in-between cases?*

- *What do your results tell you about how the proteases affect the gelatin solidification process and how heat affects the proteases?*

ExTRA

In this activity, you explored fruits that contain proteases, but many fruits do not contain proteases. You could repeat this activity using apples, blueberries, oranges, raspberries, and strawberries—all of which do not have proteases. *How well does the gelatin solidify when using fruits that do not contain proteases?*

ExTRA

Meat tenderizer contains some of the same proteases that are found in the fruits explored in this activity. Try making a gelatin dessert with meat tenderizer (by dissolving 1 teaspoon of meat tenderizer in 1 teaspoon [5 ml] of water and adding this to the 1 cup [237 ml] of gelatin liquid). *Can gelatin solidify when it is made with meat tenderizer? If a solution of meat tenderizer is heated, is the enzyme deactivated?*

⚛ SCIENCE FAIR IDEA

You used heat in this activity to inactivate the proteases in fruit, but other temperatures and conditions may inactivate the proteases as well. *Does freezing the fruit inactivate the proteases? Do other processes, such as drying or canning, inactivate the proteases?*

OBSERVATIONS AND RESULTS ·········

Did the cup with the raw fruit remain a liquid? Did the cups with the cooked fruit and no fruit added solidify like normal?

Normally the collagen proteins in gelatin form a tangled mesh that traps water and other ingredients in it, giving the gelatin its semisolid form when it cools. Proteases can cut up the proteins so that the gelatin cannot solidify. There are several different kinds of proteases in the fruits recommended for this activity, and using any of these fresh fruits should result in gelatin that does not solidify well, if at all. Heating the fruit (through boiling or steaming), however, should inactivate the proteases, and the resulting gelatin mixture should solidify like normal (or nearly normal—if the fruit was hot when the gelatin was added, the solidified gelatin may have been slightly less firm than that in the cup without fruit). The proteases bromelain and papain (which come from pineapples and papayas, respectively) are often used in meat tenderizers. There are several other fruit proteases, however, such as actinidin (from kiwi fruit) and ficin (figs).

CLEANUP ·············

You may enjoy a tasty fruit and gelatin dessert. Be sure to store it in the refrigerator until it is consumed.

THE SCIENTIFIC METHOD

The scientific method helps scientists—and students—gather facts to prove whether an idea is true. Using this method, scientists come up with ideas and then test those ideas by observing facts and drawing conclusions. You can use the scientific method to develop and test your own ideas!

Question: What do you want to learn? What problem needs to be solved? Be as specific as possible.

Research: Learn more about your topic and refine your question.

Hypothesis: Form an educated guess about what you think will answer your question. This allows you to make a prediction you can test.

Experiment: Create a test to learn if your hypothesis is correct. Limit the number of variables, or elements of the experiment that could change.

Analysis: Record your observations about the progress and results of your experiment. Then analyze your data to understand what it means.

Conclusion: Review all your data. Did the results of the experiment match the prediction? If so, your hypothesis was correct. If not, your hypothesis may need to be changed.

61

GLOSSARY

bombard: To attack a person with questions or information.

cardiovascular: Relating to the heart and the body's blood vessels.

constraint: To be restricted.

derive: To take from a source.

dilute: To water down or weaken the strength of a solution.

discrepancy: The state of being in disagreement.

entice: To attract.

mandatory: Required.

osmosis: The movement of a liquid such as water through a membrane.

pH: A number between 0 and 14 that shows if a chemical is a base or an acid. A chemical with a pH higher than 7 is a base, and a chemical with a pH lower than 7 is an acid.

palate: The sense of taste.

rancid: Having a bad, bitter taste due to not being fresh any longer.

replicate: To make a copy of something.

soluble: Able to be dissolved in a liquid.

translucent: Allowing light to pass through.

umami: The taste that has a rich, meaty flavor associated with cheese, mushrooms, cooked meat, and soy.

ADDITIONAL RESOURCES

Books

Debbink, Andrea. *Kitchen Chemistry: A Food Science Cookbook*. Middleton, WI: American Girl Publishing, 2021.

Gardy, Jennifer. *It Takes Guts: How Your Body Turns Food into Fuel (and Poop)*. Vancouver, BC, Canada: Greystone Kids, 2021.

Twiddy, Robin. *Silly Food Science*. Minneapolis, MN: Lerner Publications, 2021.

Websites

Discovery Education
sciencefaircentral.com

Exploratorium
www.exploratorium.edu/explore/activities

Science Buddies
www.sciencebuddies.org/science-fair-projects/project-ideas/list

Science Fun for Everyone!
www.sciencefun.org/?s=science+fair

Videos

Gum + Chocolate = ???
www.pbslearningmedia.org/resource/gum-chocolate-reactions/gum-chocolate-reactions/

How to Cookie with Science
www.pbslearningmedia.org/resource/cookie-with-science-reactions/cookie-with-science-reactions/

INDEX